Anatomy of a PLANE CRASH

of a

by Amie Jane Leavitt

Consultant:
Kevin Pritchard, PhD
Aeronautical Engineer
American Institute of Aeronautics
and Astronautics

CAPSTONE PRESS
a capstone imprint

Velocity is published by Capstone Press,
151 Good Counsel Drive, P.O. Box 669, Mankato, Minnesota 56002.
www.capstonepub.com

072011
006285R

 Books published by Capstone Press are manufactured with paper
containing at least 10 percent post-consumer waste.

Library of Congress Cataloging-in-Publication Data
Leavitt, Amie Jane.
  Anatomy of a plane crash / by Amie Jane Leavitt.
    p. cm. — (Velocity. disasters)
  Includes bibliographical references and index.
  Summary: "Describes the parts of an airplane, circumstances that can cause
an airplane to crash, and safety features"—Provided by publisher.
  ISBN 978-1-4296-4796-0 (library binding)
  1. Aircraft accidents—Juvenile literature. 2. Aeronautics—Safety measures—
Juvenile literature. I. Title. II. Series.
  TL553.5.L38 2011
  363.12'4—dc22   2010014604

Editorial Credits
Jennifer Fretland VanVoorst, editor; Heidi Thompson, designer;
  Svetlana Zhurkin, media researcher; Eric Manske, production specialist

Photo Credits
Alamy/Colin Underhill, 8–9; Alamy/Imagebroker, 38; AP Photo/Carlos Osorio, 28–29; AP Photo/Robert
Nichols, 24–25; AP Photo/Steven Day, 4–5; Capstone Press, 7 (bottom), 27, 40; Corbis/epa/Martial
Trezzini, 18–19; Dreamstime/Ang Wee Heng John, 43 (top); Getty Images/Bloomberg/John Cogill,
11; Getty Images/Mark Wilson, 34–35; Getty Images/Time & Life Pictures/Terry Ashe, 20–21; Getty
Images/Win McNamee, 32; iStockphoto/brytta, cover (bottom); iStockphoto/Gene Chutka, 41 (bottom);
iStockphoto/George Cairns, 26 (top); Library of Congress, 12; Newscom, 16–17, 36–37; Newscom/AFP/
Jeff Haynes, 30; Newscom/AFP/Matt Campbell, 31; Newscom/Sipa Press/Safety Reliability Methods, 5
(top); NOAA, 26 (bottom); Shutterstock/Alexander Gatsenko, 43 (bottom); Shutterstock/Barry Maas, 18
(inset); Shutterstock/Carlos E. Santa Maria, 33; Shutterstock/Christian Lagerek, 39; Shutterstock/Elena
Aliaga, 10; Shutterstock/fantastix, 13; Shutterstock/Fedor Selivanov, 6–7; Shutterstock/Filip Fuxa, cover
(top); Shutterstock/Ilja Mašík, 44–45; Shutterstock/Nikonov (metal background), throughout; Shutterstock/
Oculo (mosaic design element), cover and throughout; Shutterstock/Ramon Berk, 22–23; Shutterstock/Rob
Wilson, 42–43; Shutterstock/Sebastian Kaulitzki (scratched metal background), back cover and throughout;
Shutterstock/Stanislav E. Petrov (cement background), throughout; Shutterstock/Stubblefield Photography,
14; Shutterstock/Yung, 41 (top); Wikipedia/NTSB, 17 (bottom); Wikipedia/Plenumchamber, 15

TABLE OF CONTENTS

MIRACLE ON THE HUDSON

On January 15, 2009, at 3:26 p.m., US Airways Flight 1549 took off from New York City's La Guardia Airport. The pilot, Captain Chesley B. Sullenberger III, expected this to be a flight like any other. But as the plane began to climb, he heard loud thumps on both sides of the aircraft. "It felt like the airplane [was] being pelted by heavy rain or hail," he recalled. But the real cause was much more alarming. The plane had hit a flock of birds, and now both engines had failed. It was a pilot's worst nightmare.

Captain Sullenberger stayed calm as he contacted air traffic control. Within minutes, his plane had descended rapidly. He knew he couldn't make an airport landing. "We're gonna be in the Hudson" were the last words air traffic control heard from Sullenberger.

On board, the passengers saw flames shooting from the engines as the plane neared the Hudson River. "Brace for impact," Captain Sullenberger announced.

4

"I needed to touch down with the wings exactly level. I needed to touch down with the nose slightly up. I needed to touch down at a descent rate that was survivable. And I needed to touch down just above our minimum flying speed, but not below it. And I needed to make all these things happen **simultaneously**."

—CAPTAIN CHESLEY B. SULLENBERGER III

After the plane glided to a stop on the water, the passengers unlatched the exit doors. They rushed out onto the plane's wings. Rescue crews were already racing to the scene. Because of Captain Sullenberger's expert piloting and the quick response of emergency crews, no one died in the crash. Later, people called the landing a miracle on the Hudson.

Plane crashes are rare. That's why they receive so much media attention when they happen. But what makes some planes go down and other ones fly safely to their destinations? Let's explore the anatomy of a plane crash.

simultaneously—at the same time

Chapter 1

TAKING FLIGHT

Four forces must be kept in balance for an airplane to achieve and maintain flight.

Lift: Lift happens when air moves over and under the wings. When lift is greater than gravity, the plane is able to take off and climb.

Drag: As the air travels across the plane's body and wings, it creates friction. This force, called drag, slows down the plane.

friction—the force that slows down objects when they rub against each other

6

Thrust: Thrust is the force that pushes the airplane forward. This force works in opposition to drag. Thrust is created by an airplane's propeller or jet engines.

Gravity: Gravity is the force that pulls the airplane back down toward the earth. It works in opposition to lift. This force helps the plane descend and land. Gravity is the only force that is constant. The other three forces can be changed by the pilot.

LOW-PRESSURE AIR

AIRFOIL

An airplane's wing has a special shape called an airfoil. This shape helps to lift the plane. The air that travels over the top of the wings moves faster than the air that travels underneath them. This creates low air pressure on top of the wings and high air pressure on the bottom. Air with high pressure always moves toward air with low pressure. Because of this, the air pushes up and lifts the plane.

HIGH-PRESSURE AIR

Parts of a Plane

Many parts of an airplane work together to control thrust, lift, and drag.

propeller: The propeller is a turning blade that is powered by the engine and provides thrust. (In a jet, thrust is provided by jet engines.)

cockpit: The cockpit is where the pilot and flight crew command and control the plane.

landing gear: The plane's landing gear supports the weight of the plane when on the ground.

wings: The wings create the airplane's lift. They have two moveable controls—ailerons and flaps.

flaps: The flaps are lowered for takeoff and raised for landing. They change the surface area of the wings, affecting lift.

rudder: The rudder helps keep the plane stable in strong winds.

aileron: The aileron is made up of flaps that allow the plane to roll.

tail: The plane's tail section contains the elevator and rudder.

fuselage: The fuselage is the plane's main body.

elevator: The elevator moves up and down to keep the plane flying level.

G-BWNC

Air Traffic Control

Air traffic controllers monitor planes from the time they leave the gates to the time they arrive at their destinations. The job of air traffic control is to keep all airplanes flying over the United States safe. The controllers make sure planes are not flying in the same path in the sky. This keeps planes from colliding with each other. The controllers also monitor weather conditions. They tell the pilots if they are nearing dangerous storms or wind patterns. The controllers also help planes that are in trouble. If a pilot needs to make an emergency landing, air traffic controllers help him or her do so.

Air traffic controllers need special skills and qualities to do their important job. They have to pay attention to detail. They have to stay calm in difficult situations. They need good communication skills to tell pilots what to do.

Steps from Departure to Landing

1. Ground controller clears plane to leave the gate and directs it to the runway.

2. Local controller tells the pilot about weather conditions at the airport and clears the plane for takeoff.

3. Departure controller in airport tower guides the pilot out of the airport's airspace.

POS 15. CSU 10. EC/PLC/SASS

Air traffic controllers can see where each plane is in their airspace.

4. Enroute controllers in an air traffic control center take charge next. Teams of controllers watch all the planes that are traveling in an area. When the plane moves out of their area, another team of controllers takes over.

5. When the plane nears the airport, the pilot contacts the controllers in the tower. The controllers tell the pilot when to land.

6. After the pilot lands the plane, ground controllers help direct the plane as it **taxis** to its gate.

taxi—to move along the ground before taking off or after landing

A Risky Business

Early pilots assumed that at some point their airplanes would crash. In fact, their goal in the beginning was simply to maintain flight without crashing.

Today crashes are less common, but they still happen. So when in a flight do most accidents occur? And what must happen to a plane in order for it to crash?

The safest part of a flight is during cruise. This is when the airplane has reached its flying **altitude** and is moving at a constant speed. Takeoffs, landings, and climbs are when most accidents happen. But accidents at these parts of the flight are also the most survivable.

THE FIRST DEATH

The first death from a crash of a powered airplane was on September 17, 1908. Orville Wright was testing military planes in Fort Myer, Virginia, with U.S. Army Lieutenant Thomas Selfridge. During a flight, the right propeller of the plane broke. The plane crashed, hitting the ground nose first. Selfridge died of a broken skull. Wright suffered a broken leg and pelvis, and several broken ribs.

Phase of Flight	Percentage of Accidents	Percentage of Fatalities
Taxi	5	0
Takeoff	12	8
Initial Climb	5	14
Climb	8	25
Cruise	6	12
Descent	3	8
Initial approach	7	13
Final approach	6	16
Landing	45	2

Because of rounding, numbers do not add up to 100 percent.

altitude—the height of something above the ground

CAUSES OF CRASHES

Planes are designed with many safety features and back-up systems. For example, they can continue to fly with only one engine. When a plane crashes, it is usually because a number of things have gone wrong. Bird strikes, improper de-icing, metal fatigue, and stormy weather are some of the problems that can lead to crashes.

Bird Strikes

When a bird hits an airplane, it is called a bird strike. Bird strikes happen more often than you'd think. They usually happen at low altitudes, where birds generally fly. This means they occur most often during an airplane's takeoff or landing. From 1990 to 2007, there were nearly 80,000 reports of birds striking airplanes. But pilots are not required to report bird strikes. Therefore, the number could be much higher.

Jet engines are like giant vacuums. They pull air into a giant fan made out of large metal blades. If an object is pulled inside, it could break off one or more of these metal blades. The object and the broken blade will spin through the fan, breaking off more blades. Eventually the engine may completely shut down.

The most deadly crash that involved a bird strike happened in 1960 in Boston, Massachusetts. An Eastern Air Lines propeller plane hit a flock of birds just after takeoff. Three of the four engines stalled and the plane crashed into Boston Harbor. Sixty-two people were killed.

US Airways Flight 1549

January 15, 2009
New York, New York, to Charlotte, North Carolina

The crash of US Airways Flight 1549 was the result of a bird strike. Here are the events that led to the disaster.

3:26 p.m.
US Airways Flight 1549 takes off from La Guardia Airport. Seconds after takeoff, the pilot, Chesley B. Sullenberger III, sees birds flying toward the plane. He hears several thuds. Then he feels the engines lose thrust. Sullenberger contacts air traffic control.

3:28 p.m.
The plane's altitude has dropped from 2,800 feet (853 meters) to 1,600 feet (488 m). The pilot lowers the nose to increase speed and keep the airplane from falling from the sky. He tells air traffic control he's going to have to land in the Hudson River.

3:31 p.m.
Captain Sullenberger glides the plane onto the icy waters of the Hudson River. Passengers immediately open the exit doors. They begin climbing out onto the wings and sliding down the inflatable ramps. Minutes later, ferry boats rush to the scene. All 155 passengers and crew survive.

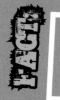

The first death in a plane crash caused by a bird strike happened in 1912 in Long Beach, California.

Airplanes are usually not damaged much by bird strikes. The amount of the damage depends on the size and number of birds involved.

But in the case of US Airways Flight 1549, the bird strike proved very dangerous. That's because the birds flew into both engines. A bird strike might disable one engine, but the chance of birds hitting both engines is very unlikely. If a bird disabled one engine, the pilot could still fly the plane on the remaining engine.

Investigators retrieved a feather from the US Airways Flight 1549 crash site.

Failure to De-ice Properly

Have you ever flown during winter? If so, you've probably seen the plane being sprayed with a clear or colored liquid just before takeoff. This is a special fluid called propylene glycol industrial grade (PGI). It melts the ice on the plane and prevents ice from forming.

Why Is De-icing Important?

An airplane's body and wings are smooth to allow air to flow across them easily. But when ice and snow build up on a plane's wings, they create a jagged surface. This buildup limits the air's ability to flow quickly over the wings. With the air speed over the wings reduced, the plane's lift is reduced.

When a plane's lift decreases, its drag increases. This drag reduces the plane's speed, causing the lift to decrease even more. With lift and speed decreasing and drag increasing, the forces that allow flight are out of balance. The plane could eventually crash.

In addition, if large chunks of ice break off during flight, they could be pulled into an engine. This could damage the blades of the fans and cause the engine to shut down.

Air Florida Flight 90
January 13, 1982
Washington, D.C., to Tampa, Florida

The crash of Air Florida Flight 90 was the result of improper de-icing. Here are the events that led to the disaster.

2:30 p.m.
After being closed for the morning because of a severe snowstorm, Washington National Airport is reopened. But weather conditions are still very poor.

3:00 p.m.
Air Florida Flight 90 is de-iced.

3:23 p.m.
Air Florida Flight 90 is cleared to leave the gate. The towing equipment can't move the plane. Instead, the captain uses reverse thrust on the engines to help push the plane back. Experts believe this allowed slush to spray on the wings and thrust sensors in the engine.

3:38 p.m.
Pilots do not turn on the engine's de-icing system. This causes the thrust sensors to send incorrect readings to the instruments.

3:47 p.m.
The copilot notices snow on the wings. The pilots decide to use the exhaust from the plane in front of them to melt the ice. This just pushes the slush to the back part of the wings, where it freezes again.

3:59 p.m.
The copilot senses that the plane is going slower than what the instruments show. He is correct. Because the thrust sensors on the engine are now frozen, the readings are wrong. The captain doesn't know this, however. He trusts that his instruments are correct and proceeds with takeoff.

4:00 p.m.

Ice and snow on the wings have slowed the airflow. This reduces the plane's lift. The nose pitches sharply upward. This shift increases drag and reduces speed. The plane only reaches 352 feet (107 m) before it starts to fall from the sky.

4:01 p.m.

Air Florida Flight 90 hits the 14th Street Bridge and crashes into the Potomac River. Only five people aboard the plane survive. Seventy-eight people, including four on the bridge, are killed.

Metal Fatigue

Imagine opening up a paperclip to a long, straight stick and then twisting it back and forth. If you continue bending the metal, it eventually breaks. This is an example of metal fatigue.

Metal fatigue occurs when metal gets worn out. Metal fatigue happens very quickly on the weak metal used to make paperclips. But over time, even the strong metal used to build airplanes can develop cracks and break.

Sources of Metal Fatigue

Chemicals: As metal objects are exposed to chemicals like salt and chlorine, they eventually start to corrode. In coastal areas, there is a lot of salt in the air. The salty air increases the corrosion in the metal body of an airplane.

Pressurization: Changing air pressure inside a plane can cause metal fatigue. Air has low pressure at high altitudes. A plane's air must be pressurized for people to breathe properly during flight. As the pressure inside the airplane changes, the plane's body expands and contracts. Over time, this expanding and contracting can cause metal fatigue.

Age: As metal gets older and weaker, small cracks start to form. These cracks grow larger over time and can eventually cause the object to fall apart.

fatigue—the state of being tired or worn out
corrode—to destroy or eat away at something
little by little

Aloha Airlines Flight 243
April 28, 1988
Hilo, Hawaii, to Honolulu, Hawaii

The crash of Aloha Airlines Flight 243 was the result of metal fatigue. Here are the events that led to the disaster.

1:00 p.m.

Aloha Airlines Flight 243 passengers are boarded. One passenger notices a crack in the fuselage. She considers saying something to the flight attendants, but decides not to.

1:25 p.m.

Aloha Airlines Flight 243 takes off from Hilo airport.

1:48 p.m.

The aircraft reaches its cruising altitude of 24,000 feet (7,315 m). Suddenly, part of the left side of the roof cracks. The air pressure inside the cabin is different from the air pressure outside the plane. The air inside the cabin pushes through the crack in an effort to balance out the two pressures. This sudden force of air leaving the plane tears an 18-foot (5.5-m) section of the roof away.

1:58 p.m.

Pilots make an emergency landing at Kahului Airport on the island of Maui. Eight passengers are injured, and one crew member dies.

TOO MANY TAKEOFFS

When the aircraft was inspected following the crash, tiny cracks were found through most of the plane's body. Investigators determined metal fatigue caused the plane to fall apart in flight. The plane was only 19 years old. However, in the islands of Hawaii, airplanes make several short flights a day. This plane had actually taken off and landed more than 89,000 times during its 19 years of service. It's the takeoffs and landings that cause the most metal fatigue on a plane. In fact, the lifespan of a plane is not measured in years. It's actually based on how many times a plane has taken off and landed.

FACT! The passengers' seatbelts kept them safely inside the plane when the roof was torn off in flight.

Flying into a Storm

Pilots must be constantly concerned about weather. They must watch for thunderstorms, blizzards, and dangerous winds throughout a flight. Pilots rely on weather information provided to them by air traffic control. Modern planes also have weather equipment on board that helps pilots fly through rough airspace.

Radar: Radar works by sending out radio waves. When these waves hit raindrops, they are reflected back to the plane. The waves that are sent out are compared with the waves that return. The difference in the two waves tells the direction and speed of the raindrops.

Lidar: Lidar uses light waves in a laser beam just like radar uses radio waves. Instead of measuring the speed of raindrops, lidar measures the speed of dust in the air. This measurement tells the speed of the wind.

Infrared: This system measures changes in temperature in front of the plane. Extreme temperature changes can cause sudden gusts of wind.

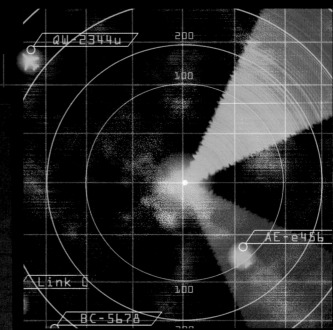

An infrared image of a hurricane off the tip of Florida uses color to show temperature differences.

Flying into a Microburst

One weather pattern that pilots watch for is a microburst. This series of wind gusts mainly affects planes during landing.

1. When a plane flies into a microburst, it encounters a strong headwind that increases its speed. The plane needs to slow down to land, so pilots reduce the thrust power in the engines.

2. The plane makes it through the headwind, but then is hit by a downdraft. This wind pushes the plane quickly toward the ground.

3. The plane then flies directly into the storm's tailwind. The tailwind blows in the same direction that the plane is flying. It pushes the plane forward very quickly. The plane is already flying low with its nose pointing downward. Therefore, a tailwind can cause the plane to crash.

1 Headwind

2 Downdraft

3 Tailwind

headwind—a wind that blows against the direction of an object

downdraft—a pocket of air that is moving downward

Delta Flight 191
August 2, 1985
Fort Lauderdale, Florida, to Dallas, Texas

The crash of Delta Flight 191 resulted from flying into a microburst. Here are the events that led to the disaster.

6:04:18 p.m.
As Delta Flight 191 prepares to land in Dallas, it encounters a thunderstorm. The pilots don't see the storm until they are already flying through it.

6:05:19 p.m.
The plane is being pounded by driving rain. Then it is hit by a gust of wind that causes it to increase speed rapidly. To slow the plane, the pilot reduces thrust from the engines.

6:05:30 p.m.
Speed returns to normal. It appears as if the plane is through the worst part of the storm. But then the plane is suddenly pushed downward.

FACT

Some airlines have stopped using the number 191 to name their flights. Why? Since 1967 there have been five flights with the number 191 that have crashed, causing numerous deaths.

6:05:44 p.m.

The pilot gives the engines full power. He is trying to pick up speed and gain altitude. But his efforts are unsuccessful.

6:05:52 p.m.

The plane is just short of the runway when it dips down and hits a field. It bounces up and then flies toward a highway. The plane's engines hit a car, killing the driver instantly.

6:05:55 p.m.

The plane bounces several more times. On the last bounce, the plane skids along the ground and strikes two water tanks. Only 27 people survive. One hundred thirty-seven lives are lost.

The wreckage of Delta Flight 191 remained near the runway while federal investigators studied the crash. Departing planes had to fly over the crash site.

Chapter 3

AFTERMATH AND RECOVERY

After an airplane crashes, investigators rush to the scene. Here's who they are and what they do.

NTSB: In the United States, the National Transportation Safety Board (NTSB) investigates transportation–related accidents. When the NTSB investigates a crash, it brings a variety of experts to the scene. These experts collect data to help determine the cause of the crash. They look at the plane's history to see if any problems could have caused the accident. Sometimes it takes months for these experts to finish their investigations.

FAA: If a crash has no deaths and involves a small plane, the Federal Aviation Administration (FAA) may investigate. The FAA is part of the U.S. government. It is in charge of air traffic control and airport security. It also makes and enforces rules for mechanics, pilots, airplanes, and airports.

FBI: Sometimes a crash is believed to have been caused by a criminal act. In such a case, agents from the Federal Bureau of Investigation (FBI) are the first on the scene. They gather the information needed to identify and take legal action against those responsible for the crash.

The Black Box

The black box is one of the most important items on the plane for investigators to study. The black box is housed in the back of the plane near the tail. It has the greatest chance of remaining undamaged in this part of the aircraft. When a plane crashes, it usually dives forward nose first. If the plane crashes this way, the tail section would have the least amount of damage.

Because of its name, you'd assume the black box is black in color. It's not. It's painted neon orange with white reflecting strips strapped around its surface. The box's color helps search crews locate it more easily at a crash site.

Honeywell
FLIGHT
RECORDER
DO NOT OPEN

On most commercial airplanes, there are two black boxes. One is the flight data recorder (FDR). The other is the cockpit voice recorder (CVR). Each black box records different information about the flight.

The FDR records details about the plane's mechanics. It monitors data such as speed, altitude, fuel flow, and direction.

Black boxes were first installed in airplanes in the 1950s. By the 1960s, these recording devices were required on all aircraft in the United States.

Pilots' conversations in the cockpit can reveal information about the cause of a plane crash.

The CVR records all of the sounds in the cockpit. This includes all of the conversation between the flight crew. It also includes any other sounds from this part of the plane. When investigators study the CVR after a crash, they listen to the tape many times. They listen for any sound that might give them a clue about what caused the crash.

Steps of an NTSB Investigation

Step 1: Technical Investigation

NTSB's "Go Team" is on the scene of a plane crash within hours. This group of investigators starts combing through the wreckage looking for information. They collect parts of the plane that may have come off along the plane's route. This wreckage is then used to piece the plane back together like a giant jigsaw puzzle. Each investigator later leads a team that studies the different parts of the crash.

Step 2: Turn in Reports

Once the groups are finished with their investigation, they describe their findings. Their reports are turned in to the NTSB.

Step 3: Public Hearing

The NTSB conducts a public hearing to discuss all of the reports. Experts, pilots, air traffic controllers, survivors, engineers, and witnesses may be asked to speak.

Step 4: Release Official Report

The NTSB reviews all of the information from the public hearing. Then it releases an official report.

Step 5: Further Review

In some cases, a group may not be satisfied with the NTSB's report. The group can ask the board to review the information again. For example, the pilot might be found responsible for the crash. Then the pilot's union might ask the board to further review the data.

Step 6: Final Report

If the NTSB decides that changes are needed, they are made for the final report. In this report, the NTSB describes the facts of the accident. It concludes why the accident most likely happened and recommends ways to improve safety on future flights.

Problems and Solutions

The airline industry in the United States has improved a great deal over the years. Many of these improvements have been made because of the lessons learned from plane crashes.

Air Traffic Control System

In 1956, TWA Flight 2 and United Flight 718 collided over the Grand Canyon. The crash killed every person on board both planes. Because of this, the United States spent $250 million to improve its air traffic control system. The air traffic controllers can now see where every plane is in the air. No commercial planes have collided in the United States since then.

Smoke Detectors

In 1983, an electrical fire started behind the bathroom walls of Air Canada Flight 797. There was no smoke detector in the bathroom. The flight crew didn't find out about the fire until it was too late. No one died in the crash. Still, the smoke and fire ended up killing half the people on board. Every plane now has smoke detectors installed in its bathrooms.

Aisle Lighting

Today aisle lighting on the floor of the cabin is standard in all commercial airliners. Air Canada Flight 797 didn't have this lighting. When the plane crashed, the smoke and lack of light kept the passengers from finding the exits quickly. Many died as a result.

INSIDE AN AIR TRAFFIC CONTROL TOWER

De-icing Procedures

After Air Florida Flight 90's crash, the FAA made stricter rules for de-icing planes. It also created new guidelines for flying in winter weather.

Improved Pilot Training

In 1977, Southern Airways Flight 242 crashed in New Hope, Georgia. The plane had flown through a violent thunderstorm and its engines had been damaged by hail. Seventy-two people were killed, including the pilots and some people on the ground. Because of this crash, pilots received better training on how to fly in storms.

Pilots use flight simulators to help them learn and practice new techniques for flying in storms.

Weather Radar Equipment

After Delta Flight 191 crashed in a microburst, the FAA improved the type of radar installed on aircraft. The new radar equipment lets pilots know when they are flying into a microburst. Better weather forecasting equipment is also used at both the airport and air traffic control centers.

Inspection of Older Aircraft

The fate of Aloha Flight 243 prompted the FAA to create stricter inspection guidelines for older aircraft. Planes are inspected regularly. Inspectors look for even the tiniest cracks in the body, wings, propellers, and engines. Inspectors know that even a small crack can cause an enormous disaster.

Chapter 4

DESIGNED FOR SAFETY

An airplane is designed so that passengers can **evacuate** quickly in case of an emergency. Every plane has to have enough exits that all passengers can evacuate within 90 seconds. Most planes have exits at the front, over the wings, and at the back.

Exits at the front and back of the plane have inflatable ramps. These ramps help people get down from the plane to the ground or water below. The people who exit in the middle can just climb out onto the wings.

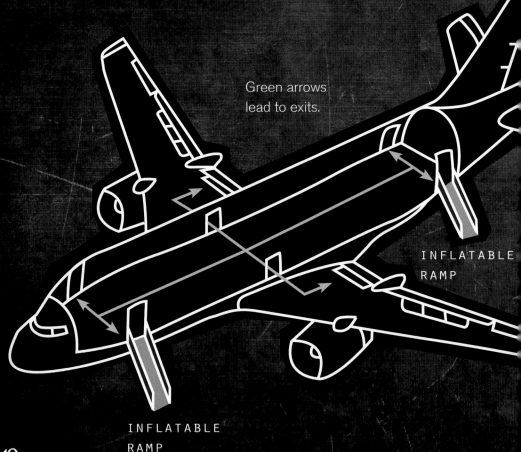

Green arrows lead to exits.

INFLATABLE RAMP

INFLATABLE RAMP

Seatbelts: Every seat has a seatbelt. Just like in a car, you are much safer with your seatbelt on than if you aren't wearing it.

Life Jackets and Flotation Devices: Under every seat is a life jacket. Your seat cushion can also be used as a flotation device if the plane lands in water.

Oxygen Masks: Every seat has an oxygen mask in the ceiling above it. The masks will drop down if there is smoke in the cabin or if the oxygen level decreases.

Safety Instruction Cards: Every seat has an instruction card showing how to use all of the plane's safety devices. Pay attention to the flight attendants when they demonstrate these features before takeoff. The information they give you could save your life in a crash.

evacuate—to move away from an area because it is dangerous there

Survival Tips

A SURVIVOR'S STORY

Larry Snodgrass was a passenger on US Airways Flight 1549 when it crashed in New York's Hudson River. He spoke of the importance of staying calm in an emergency and helping others. "Every man I saw started helping ladies out, the kids," he said. "Almost everybody seemed more concerned with the person on their left or right. ... It was all surprisingly calm." It is important to stay calm in an emergency. The calm attitude of the passengers on US Airways Flight 1549 may have helped save their lives.

Choose the best clothing: What you wear can make a difference in surviving a plane crash. Wear clothes and shoes that are comfortable and that allow you to move freely. Long sleeves and pants offer more protection than a tank top and shorts. Athletic shoes provide a more secure footing than flip-flops.

Look around you: When you take your seat, look around for the nearest exit. It's a good idea to count the number of rows between your seat and the exit. If you have to get off in the dark, you can find your way to the exit easier.

◀EXIT▶

Select the best seat: If you can choose your seat, sit in an exit row or within five rows of one. The closer you are to an exit, the faster you can evacuate in an emergency. Aisle seats are also better than window seats.

Dangerous, but Rare

When an airplane crashes, it makes headline news. Airplane accidents are a frightening thought for many people. Yet part of the reason why they receive so much press is because they hardly ever happen.

In one year, more than 64 million planes take off in the United States alone. Of those planes, about 10 million are scheduled flights by the airlines. Check out how many scheduled airline flights in the United States crashed between 2002 and 2008.

Year	Total Accidents	Fatal Accidents	Total Fatalities	Total Fatalities on Board
2002	34	0	0	0
2003	51	2	22	21
2004	23	1	13	13
2005	34	3	22	20
2006	27	2	50	49
2007	26	0	0	0
2008	20	0	0	0

Every day, more than 87,000 planes fly the skies of the United States.

Look at the information for 2008. Of the 10 million airline flights that took off and landed, there were only 20 accidents. And of those 20 accidents, no one died. Those are some good odds.

Air travel is one of the safest forms of transportation. With improvements being made all the time, it is only getting safer.

GLOSSARY

altitude (AL-ti-tood)—the height of something above the ground

corrode (kuh-RODE)—to destroy or eat away at something little by little

downdraft (DOUN-draft)—a pocket of air that is moving downward

evacuate (i-VAK-yoo-ate)—to move away from an area because it is dangerous there

fatigue (fuh-TEEG)—the state of being tired or worn out

friction (FRIK-shun)—the force that slows down objects when they rub against each other

headwind (HED-wind)—a wind that blows against the direction of an object

infrared (IN-fruh-red)—a system that uses heat energy to detect and locate objects

lidar (LYE-dar)—a system that uses light waves to detect and locate objects

radar (RAY-dar)—a system that uses radio waves to detect and locate objects

simultaneously (sye-muhl-TAY-nee-uhss-lee)—at the same time

taxi (TAK-see)—to move along the ground before taking off or after landing

READ MORE

Eason, Sarah. *How Does a Jet Plane Work?* How Does It Work? New York: Gareth Stevens Pub., 2010.

Langley, Andrew. *Planes.* Machines on the Move. Mankato, Minn.: Amicus, 2011.

Spalding, Frank. *Plane Crash: True Stories of Survival.* Survivor Stories. New York.: Rosen Central, 2007.

West, David. *Plane.* Why Things Don't Work. Chicago: Raintree, 2007.

INTERNET SITES

FactHound offers a safe, fun way to find Internet sites related to this book. All of the sites on FactHound have been researched by our staff.

Here's all you do:

Visit *www.facthound.com*

Type in this code: 9781429647960

INDEX